Dedication

This book is dedicated to my brave daughter, Mackenzie, who has gone through more in her life then I can ever imagine. She is one of the strongest, scratch that, the strongest person that I have ever met. Together we wrote this book to help her prepare for her upcoming surgeries and in the process she decided to share her story to help other kids just like her. I admire her strength, compassion and empathy. She has taught me so much. To her I say Thank you! More than the sun and the moon and the stars above, I love you, Always and Forever!

Love,

Mom

Acknowledgements

To the Doctors and Nurses at Toronto's Hospital for Sick Children and Dr. Diane Sacks, there are no words to express our gratitude; we are forever in your debt. To the Child Life team, thank you for keeping things "normal" and allowing Mackenzie to be a kid. Thank you to Dr. Wendy Le Doux, for giving us the idea and courage to put our thoughts to paper. And to our friends and family, thank you for all your strength, support and love, you are what kept us going...Thank you, we love you <3

Finally, to those reading, We wish you well and send you strength and support in these pages. Thank you and Good luck on your journey!

Hi! My name is Mackenzie and I am 7 years old. I was born with a hole in my heart. This is called a birth defect and sometimes you need surgery to fix them. I don't call it a defect though, I don't really call it anything, I just wish I didn't have "an oops" but I do, and in my case I have had, and will need more surgery to fix it.

I have already had 3 heart surgeries and 8 "Cardiac catheters" (these are kinda like mini surgeries where the doctors go into my heart through arteries....I don't fully understand the how but the getting ready for them is the same as surgery). I have another "cath" coming up very soon. Even though I have had surgeries before I still get scared and that's ok. It's normal to be scared.

If you are reading this book maybe you have a heart defect or some other problem that will need the doctors to help make you better.

.

Maybe you will need a surgery or surgeries to fix it and I know that that can be very scary but it will be ok. Maybe you even had some surgeries before, and like me, were very young and don't remember. If you had surgery when you were very little this time it might seem like the very first time even though it isn't. I know I have to have these surgeries because they are saving my life and even though they are scary I want to have them so I can get better. Ok I don't "want" to have them but I want to be here and I got through them and I know you will too! I'm here to tell you, whether it's the first time or the 8th time I know it's still scary, but it will be ok and you will be better than ever!

Let's begin.......

The first question I had was, why did this happen…why was I born with a hole in my heart? A lot of times we don't really know the answer but that doesn't help you feel better so this is how my mom explained it to me….she said it was kinda like having the hiccups.

Everyone gets hiccups and sometimes if we're talking it makes the words come out funny. Well, birth defects are kinda like your body hiccupping while you are growing in your mommy's tummy.

With me, my body hiccupped when my heart was growing. Instead of saying the word "heart" it hiccupped and came out "he_rt", not quite the full word and I was born with a hole in my heart. Sometimes we get hiccups and we don't know why but we do. Everyone has some hiccup, sometimes they are little but sometimes they are big and loud and need help from doctors to go away. This is a story of how we helped fix my hiccup. I hope it helps you know that you are not alone and however long or short your journey is you will get there.

There are lots of people in my life that love me and are on this journey with me so I know I am not alone and neither are you. All these people are on my team to help me and we all work together so that I get better. You might not know this but you have a team too!

Let's look at your team together. There are all your doctors, nurses and surgeons that help make your body better and then there are your parents, your sisters or brothers, aunts/uncles, grandparents, friends, the "child life" team (mine are Alison and Katie) and the list goes on. Each of these people love you and are there to help you in many ways. They are there to talk to, answer questions, and give hugs when you are scared or just to play with you and have fun with. Stop and think about your team, you'll be surprised how fast it grows!

So now that we have our team, it's time to start getting ready for the big day. This means some visits to the hospital. At these visits there will be lots of talking, which I think is boring but it helps mom, dad and the doctors to know what is happening and what you need. It is where you can ask any questions or talk about any worries that you might have. Don't be afraid to ask anytime you think of them either though. It's always good to ask questions if you have them. It is also here that if you think you will still be scared on the day of surgery you can ask for some special medicine that you can take that will help you relax and not be scared.

The visits will not just be talking, there are also tests that you will need, these aren't boring but they aren't a lot of fun either and sometimes even a little scary. But they are often very fast so it's done quickly. You might need x-rays, these are just pictures with a special camera that can see inside your body and that's pretty cool!

You may also need blood work. This is a needle and that might sound scary but it's so fast and I try to think about something else, like remembering my trips to my cottage and building sand castles. You should try thinking of your favorite place. Close your eyes and pretend you are there, remember all the things about this favorite place, the smell, the sound, what you are doing…..WOW look the blood work is done! I bet you didn't even feel it!

SPLASH!!!!!!

SPLASH!!!!!!

You may have other tests too in preparation for your surgery but I bet you are really really brave and can get through those too. If you have any questions about any of them don't be afraid to ask them. Having answers helps me not be afraid. And remember, if you still feel scared or nervous about the test close your eyes and go to your favorite place......I'm going to the beach. It's beautiful and sunny and warm. I love to swim! Sometimes my favorite place is just at home too. Where is your place? Close your eyes and think about it now....what do you see, what are you doing, what can you smell? Wow I bet it's wonderful there!

With all your tests done it's now the night before surgery. What you will have learned during one of the talking times is that surgery has to be done on an empty stomach. This means no eating from bedtime the night before and no breakfast the next morning. This makes me worried that I will be hungry so I make sure to ask my mom and dad for my favorite dinner. And the best part is the snack before bed, which for me is sometimes just more dinner and sometimes it's a special dessert! What's your favorite dinner?

In the morning I have to get up sooo early, it's still dark! Then we drive to the hospital and check in. We get to go to "our" room and the nurse comes in for a couple more tests. Don't worry these are easy!

First they check how much you weigh, and after that special dinner maybe you've gained a few pounds, you should check. Hop on!

Then they check your blood pressure, that's just a little hug for your arm. It's fast but you have to remember to stay very still. The nurse may also want to check your temperature and listen to your heart too.

After that the nurse will give you a funny sponge and you get to have a quick bath or shower with it, it feels cool, even tickles. Then you get to put on special hospital clothes, these are just so your clothes stay clean. This is also the time the nurse may give you the special medicine to help you not be scared. After that…it's time to just wait to be called…..make sure you bring colouring books or something to play with. Don't forget your special "stuffy" if you have one, he can come with you to the operating room……I'm bringing "George".

When they call you, you might go into another room to wait or you might be going straight to surgery. Your mom and dad can't be in the room with you during surgery but they will be there until it's time to go and during surgery they will be close by waiting for you in a special room. If you haven't had the special medicine, this is when I start getting nervous again...so I close my eyes and go to my favorite place.....remember yours?

You are asleep for the surgery so you don't feel it or really even know it's happening. To get me to sleep I used to have a mask with special "air" that is flavoured, I got watermelon! This time I am going to use the IV instead. The IV is just like a little needle and we've done that lots of times and know it's very fast. With the IV, the needle goes out but a tube stays in your hand. The doctors use this tube to give your body drinks while you are sleeping…they also use this tube to give you medicine. This time they are going to use the IV tube to give me medicine to make me go to sleep the same way the special "air" does with the mask. I'm getting sleepy………..

It's time……zzzzzzzzzz

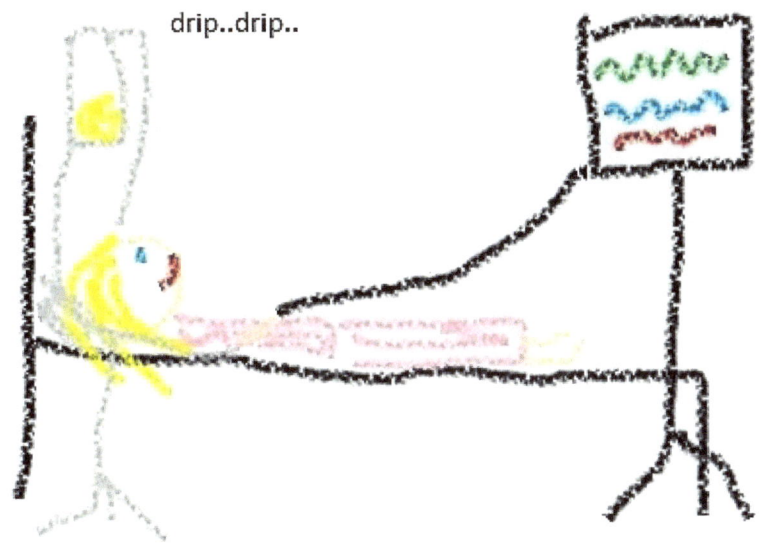

When I wake up the surgery is all done. I didn't even feel it at all! I don't remember the surgery because I was sleeping. I still feel a little tired and my throat is a little sore but that means I get freezies! There are lots of wires on me and machines around me making noises. I used to think the noises and beeps were scary because I thought it meant there was something wrong but my mom says it's just the machines talking to the doctors and it's ok. Now I'm not so scared….but they are annoying.

You may have to stay overnight or for a few nights in the hospital just to make sure you rest but I don't mind it, secretly its kinda fun staying…..there are movies and games and crafts I can do. If I feel good I can go to the playroom but if I want to stay in my room they can bring the stuff to me! I even get room service, that's where they bring the food right to your bed!

Each day you're there the doctors or nurses will take away some of the wires and tubes.
Sometimes I feel scared when they are removing a bandage or the IV but just remember each one
that is removed is a step closer to going home. Then, when you are strong enough the doctors
will tell you it's time to go home! Yay!

Some parts of the journey have been scary but I have been very very brave just like you and now I feel much better. I know that even though I have another surgery and I still get a little scared I will feel even better after this one too! I know I have a great team around me, just like you, and I will be ok, even better then ok, I am me and I am GREAT!!

I am now 9 years old, it's been about 2 years since I wrote this book. I am in grade four and doing great in school. I love dancing and singing and especially swimming, I just finished my level 3!!!

www.ingramcontent.com/pod-product-compliance
Lightning Source LLC
Chambersburg PA
CBHW060822290526
45792CB00005BB/1765